LIBRETTO

Ruddigore

or
The Witch's Curse

© 2007 by Faber Music Ltd
First published by International Music Publications Ltd
International Music Publications Ltd is a Faber Music company
Bloomsbury House 74–77 Great Russell Street London WC1B 3DA
Printed in England by Caligraving Ltd

ISBN10: 0-571-52900-3
EAN13: 978-0-571-52900-1

To buy Faber Music publications or to find out about the full range of titles available,
please contact your local music retailer or Faber Music sales enquiries:

Faber Music Ltd, Burnt Mill, Elizabeth Way, Harlow, CM20 2HX England
Tel: +44(0)1279 82 89 82   Fax: +44(0)1279 82 89 83
sales@fabermusic.com   fabermusic.com

DRAMATIS PERSONÆ
MORTALS

SIR RUTHVEN MURGATROYD *Disguised as Robin Oakapple, a Young Farmer*

RICHARD DAUNTLESS *His Foster-Brother—A Man-o'-war's-man*

SIR DESPARD MURGATROYD *of Ruddigore. A Wicked Baronet*

OLD ADAM GOODHEART *Robin's Faithful Servant*

ROSE MAYBUD *A Village Maiden*

MAD MARGARET

DAME HANNAH *Rose's Aunt*

ZORAH
RUTH *Professional Bridesmaids*

GHOSTS

SIR RUPERT MURGATROYD *The First Baronet*

SIR JASPER MURGATROYD *The Third Baronet*

SIR LIONEL MURGATROYD *The Sixth Baronet*

SIR CONRAD MURGATROYD *The Twelfth Baronet*

SIR DESMOND MURGATROYD *The Sixteenth Baronet*

SIR GILBERT MURGATROYD *The Eighteenth Baronet*

SIR MERVYN MURGATROYD *The Twentieth Baronet*

AND

SIR RODERIC MURGATROYD *The Twenty-first Baronet*

CHORUS OF OFFICERS, ANCESTORS, PROFESSIONAL BRIDESMAIDS, AND VILLAGERS.

ACT I
The Fishing Village of Rederring, in Cornwall.

ACT II
The Picture Gallery in Ruddigore Castle.

TIME
Early in the 19th century.

MUSICAL NUMBERS

ACT I

ACT II

RUDDIGORE
or
THE WITCH'S CURSE

ACT I

SCENE—*The fishing village of Rederring (in Cornwall). ROSE MAYBUD'S cottage is seen L.*

Enter CHORUS OF BRIDESMAIDS. They range themselves in front of ROSE'S cottage.

Music No. 1.   CHORUS OF BRIDESMAIDS—(Solo Soprano, Zorah)

"Fair is Rose"

BRIDESMAIDS

CHORUS OF BRIDESMAIDS

Fair is Rose as bright May-day;
Soft is Rose as warm west-wind;
Sweet is Rose as new-mown hay—
Rose is queen of maiden-kind!
Rose, all glowing
With virgin blushes, say—
Is anybody going
To marry you to-day?

Solo—Zorah

Ev'ry day, as the days roll on,
Bridesmaids' garb we gaily don,
Sure that a maid so fairly famed
Can't long remain unclaimed
Hour by hour and day by day
Sev'ral months have passed away,
Though she's the fairest flow'r that blows,
No one has married Rose!

CHORUS

Rose, all glowing
With virgin blushes, say—
Is anybody going
To marry you to-day?

ZORAH

Hour by hour and day by day
Months have pass'd away.

CHORUS

Fair is Rose as bright May day;
Soft is Rose as warm west-wind,
Sweet is Rose as new-mown hay
Rose is Queen of maiden-kind!
Rose, all glowing
With virgin blushes, say—
Is anybody going
To marry you today?

CHORUS (Contd.)	Fair is Rose, Soft is Rose, Rose is the Queen of maiden-kind!

Enter HANNAH, *from cottage*

HANNAH	Nay, gentle maidens, you sing well but vainly, for Rose is still heart-free, and looks but coldly upon her many suitors.
ZORAH	It's very disappointing. Every young man in the village is in love with her, but they are appalled by her beauty and modesty, and won't declare themselves; so, until she makes her own choice, there's no chance for anybody else.
RUTH	This is, perhaps, the only village in the world that possesses an endowed corps of professional bridesmaids who are bound to be on duty every day from ten to four—and it is at least six months since our services were required. The pious charity by which we exist is practically wasted!
ZORAH	We shall be disendowed—that will be the end of it! Dame Hannah—you're a nice old person—*you* could marry if you liked. There's old Adam—Robin's faithful servant—he loves you with all the frenzy of a boy of fourteen.
HANNAH	Nay—that may never be, for I am pledged!
ALL	To whom?
HANNAH	To an eternal maidenhood! Many years ago I was betrothed to a god-like youth who woo'd me under an assumed name. But on the very day upon which our wedding was to have been celebrated, I discovered that he was no other than Sir Roderic Murgatroyd, one of the bad Baronets of Ruddigore, and the uncle of the man who now bears that title. As a son of that accursed race he was no husband for an honest girl, so, madly as I loved him, I left him then and there. He died but ten years since, but I never saw him again.
ZORAH	But why should you not marry a bad Baronet of Ruddigore?
RUTH	All baronets are bad; but was he worse than other baronets?
HANNAH	My child, he was accursed!
ZORAH	But who cursed him? Not you, I trust!
HANNAH	The curse is on all his line and has been, ever since the time of Sir Rupert, the first Baronet. Listen, and you shall hear the legend.

2

| Music No. 2 | SONG—(Hannah) and CHORUS |
| | |

"Sir Rupert Murgatroyd his leisure"

HANNAH

Sir Rupert Murgatroyd
His leisure and his riches
He ruthlessly employ'd
In persecuting witches.
With fear he'd make them quake—
He'd duck them in his lake—
He'd break their bones
With sticks and stones,
And burn them at the stake!

CHORUS

This sport he much enjoy'd.
Did Rupert Murgatroyd—
No sense of shame
Or pity came
To Rupert Murgatroyd!

HANNAH

Once, on the village green,
A palsied hag he roasted,
And what took place, I ween,
Shook his composure boasted,
For, as the torture grim
Seized on each withered limb,
The writhing dame
'Mid fire and flame
Yelled forth this curse on him:—
"Each lord of Ruddigore,
Despite his best endeavour,
Shall do one crime, or more,
Once, ev'ry day, for ever!
This doom he can't defy
However he may try,
For should he stay
His hand, that day
In torture he shall die!"
The prophecy came true:
Each heir who held the title
Had, ev'ry day, to do
Some crime of import vital;
Until, with guilt o'erplied,
"I'll sin no more!" he cried,
And on the day
He said that say,
In agony he died!

CHORUS

And thus, with sinning cloyed,
Has died each Murgatroyd,
And so shall fall,
Both one and all,
Each coming Murgatroyd!
[Exeunt CHORUS OF BRIDESMAIDS.

3

Enter ROSE MAYBUD from cottage, with small basket on her arm.

HANNAH	Whither away, dear Rose? On some errand of charity, as is thy wont?
ROSE	A few gifts, dear Aunt, for deserving villagers. Lo, here is some peppermint rock for old gaffer Gadderby, a set of false teeth for pretty little Ruth Rowbottom, and a pound of snuff for the poor orphan girl on the hill.
HANNAH	Ah, Rose, pity that so much goodness should not help to make some gallant youth happy for life! Rose, why dost thou harden that little heart of thine? Is there none hereaway whom thou could'st love?
ROSE	And if there were such an one, verily it would ill become me to tell him so.
HANNAH	Nay, dear one, where true love is, there is little need of prim formality.
ROSE	Hush, dear aunt, for thy words pain me sorely. Hung in a plated dish-cover to the knocker of the workhouse door, with naught that I could call mine own, save a change of baby-linen and a book of etiquette, little wonder if I have always regarded that work as a voice from a parent's tomb. This hallowed volume (*producing a book of etiquette*), composed, if I may believe the title-page, by no less an authority than the wife of a Lord Mayor, has been, through life, my guide and monitor. By its solemn precepts I have learnt to test the moral worth of all who approach me. The man who bites his bread, or eats peas with a knife, I look upon as a lost creature, and he who has not acquired the proper way of entering and leaving a room is the object of my pitying horror. There are those in this village who bite their nails, dear aunt, and nearly all are wont to use their pocket combs in public places. In truth I could pursue this painful theme much further, but behold, I have said enough.
HANNAH	But is there not one among them who is faultless, in thine eyes? For example—young Robin. He combines the manners of a Marquis with the morals of a Methodist. Could'st thou not love *him?*
ROSE	And even if I could, how should I confess it unto him? For lo, he is shy, and sayeth nought!

Music No. 3.	SONG—(Rose)
	"If somebody there chanced to be"
ROSE	If somebody there chanced to be Who loved me in a manner true, My heart would point him out to me, And I would point him out to you.
(*Referring to book.*)	But here it says of those who point, Their manners must be out of joint— You *may* not point— You *must* not point—

4

ROSE (Contd.)	It's manners out of joint, to point! Ah! Had I the love of such as he, Some quiet spot he'd take me to, Then he could whisper it to me, And I could whisper it to you. (*Referring to book*) But whispering, I've somewhere met, Is contrary to etiquette: Where can it be? (*Searching book*) Now let me see— (*Finding reference*) Yes, Yes! It's contrary to etiquette! (*Showing it to* HANNAH) If any well-bred youth I knew, Polite and gentle, neat and trim, Then I would hint as much to you, And you could hint as much to him. (*Referring to book*) But here it says, in plainest print, "It's most unladylike to hint"— You *may* not hint, You *must* not hint— It says you mustn't hint, in print! Ah! And if I loved him through and through— (True love and not a passing whim), Then I could speak of it to you, And you could speak of it to him. But here I find it doesn't do To speak until you're spoken to. (*Referring to book*) Where can it be? (*Searching book*) Now let me see— (*Finding reference*) Yes, yes! "Don't speak until you're spoken to"!

Exit HANNAH.

ROSE	Poor Aunt! Little did the good soul think, when she breathed the hallowed name of Robin, that he would do even as well as another. But he resembleth all the youths in this village, in that he is unduly bashful in my presence, and lo, it is hard to bring him to the point. But soft, he is here!

(ROSE is about to go when ROBIN enters and calls her)

ROBIN	Mistress Rose!
ROSE	(*Surprised*) Master Robin!
ROBIN	I wished to say that—it is fine.
ROSE	It is passing fine.
ROBIN	But we do want rain.
ROSE	Aye, sorely! Is that all?
ROBIN	(*Sighing*) That is all.

ROSE	Good day, Master Robin!
ROBIN	Good day, Mistress Rose! (*Both going—both stop*)
ROSE **ROBIN**	⎰ I crave pardon, I— ⎱ I beg pardon, I—
ROSE	You were about to say?—
ROBIN	I would fain consult you—
ROSE	Truly?
ROBIN	It is about a friend.
ROSE	In truth I have a friend myself.
ROBIN	Indeed? I mean, of course—
ROSE	And I would fain consult you—
ROBIN	(*Anxiously*) About him?
ROSE	(*Prudishly*) About *her*.
ROBIN	(*Relieved*) Let us consult one another.

Music No. 4.	DUET—(ROSE and ROBIN)
	"I know a youth"
ROBIN	I know a youth who loves a little maid— (Hey, but his face is a sight for to see!) Silent is he, for he's modest and afraid— (Hey, but he's timid as a youth can be!)
ROSE	I know a maid who loves a gallant youth, (Hey, but she sickens as the days go by!) She cannot tell him all the sad, sad truth— (Hey, but I think that little maid will die!)
ROBIN	Poor little man!
ROSE	Poor little maid!
ROBIN	Poor little man!
ROSE	Poor little maid!
BOTH	Now tell me pray, and tell me true, What in the world should the ⎰ young man ⎱ do? ⎱ maiden ⎰

6

ROBIN	He cannot eat and he cannot sleep— (Hey, but his face is a sight for to see!) Daily he goes for to wail—for to weep (Hey, but he's wretched as a youth can be!)
ROSE	She's very thin and she's very pale— (Hey, but she sickens as the days go by!) Daily she goes for to weep—for to wail— (Hey, but I think that little maid will die!)
ROBIN	Poor little maid!
ROSE	Poor little man!
ROBIN	Poor little maid!
ROSE	Poor little man!

BOTH Now tell me pray, and tell me true,

What in the world should the $\left\{\begin{array}{l}\text{young man} \\ \text{maiden}\end{array}\right\}$ do?

ROSE	If I were the youth I should offer her my name— (Hey, but her face is a sight for to see!)
ROBIN	If I were the maid I should fan his honest flame— (Hey, but he's bashful as a youth can be!)
ROSE	If I were the youth I should speak to her to-day— (Hey, but she sickens as the days go by!)
ROBIN	If I were the maid I should meet the lad half way— (For I really do believe that timid youth will die!)
ROSE	Poor little man!
ROBIN	Poor little maid!
ROSE	Poor little man!
ROBIN	Poor little maid!

BOTH I thank you, $\left\{\begin{array}{l}\text{miss,} \\ \text{sir,}\end{array}\right\}$ for your counsel true;

I'll tell that $\left\{\begin{array}{l}\text{youth} \\ \text{maid}\end{array}\right\}$ what $\left\{\begin{array}{l}\text{he} \\ \text{she}\end{array}\right\}$ ought to do.

Exit ROSE

ROBIN	Poor child! I sometimes think that if she wasn't quite so particular I might venture—but no, no—even then I should be unworthy of her!

7

(He sits desponding. Enter OLD ADAM)

ADAM   My kind master is sad! Dear Sir Ruthven Murgatroyd—

ROBIN   Hush! As you love me, breathe not that hated name. Twenty years ago, in horror at the prospect of inheriting that hideous title, and with it the ban that compels all who succeed to the baronetcy to commit at least one deadly crime per day, for life, I fled my home, and concealed myself in this innocent village under the name of Robin Oakapple. My younger brother, Despard, believing me to be dead, succeeded to the title and its attendant curse. For twenty years I have been dead and buried. Don't dig me up now.

ADAM   Dear master, it shall be as you wish, for have I not sworn to obey you for ever in all things? Yet, as we are here alone, and as I belong to that particular description of good old man to whom the truth is a refreshing novelty, let me call you by your own right title once more! (ROBIN *assents*) Sir Ruthven Murgatroyd! Baronet! Of Ruddigore! Whew! It's like eight hours at the sea-side!

ROBIN   My poor old friend! Would there were more like you!

ADAM   Would there were indeed! But I bring you good tidings. Your foster-brother, Richard, has returned from sea—his ship the Tom-Tit rides yonder at anchor, and he himself is even now in this very village!

ROBIN   My beloved foster-brother? No, no—it cannot be!

ADAM   It is even so—and see, he comes this way

(Exeunt together)
(Enter Chorus of Bridesmaids)

Music Nos. 5 & 6   CHORUS OF BRIDESMAIDS AND SONG—(Richard)

"From the briny sea"

BRIDESMAIDS   From the briny sea
Comes young Richard, all victorious!
Valorous is he—
His achievements all are glorious!
Let the welkin ring
With the news we bring,
Sing it—shout it—
Tell about it—shout it!
Safe and sound returneth he,
All victorious from the sea!
SOPRANOS
Safe
and
sound,
All victorious
from the sea!

CONTRALTOS
Safe and sound re—
turneth
he,
All victorious
from the sea!

8

Enter RICHARD. The girls welcome him as he greets old acquaintances.

BALLAD—RICHARD

I shipp'd, d'ye see, in a Revenue sloop,
And, off Cape Finistere,
A merchantman we see,
A Frenchman, going free,
So we made for the bold Mounseer,
D'ye see?
We made for the bold Mounseer.
But she proved to be a Frigate—and she up with her ports,
And fires with a thirty-two!
It come uncommon near,
But we answer'd with a cheer,
Which paralysed the Parly-voo!
D'ye see?
Which paralysed the Parly-voo,

BRIDESMAIDS   Which paralysed the Parly-voo, D'ye see?
Which paralysed the Parly-voo!

RICHARD   Then our Capt'n he up and he says, says he,
"That chap we need not fear,—
We can take her, if we like,
She is sartin for to strike,
For she's only a darned Mounseer!
D'ye see?
She's only a darned Mounseer!
But to fight a French fal-lal—it's like hittin' of a gal—
It's a lubberly thing for to do;

For we, with all our faults,
Why we're sturdy British salts,
While she's only a poor Parly-voo,
D'ye see?
While she's only a poor Parly-voo!"

BRIDESMAIDS   While she's only a poor Parly-voo, D'ye see?
While she's only a poor Parly-voo!

RICHARD   So we up with our helm, and we scuds before the breeze,
As we gives a compassionating cheer;
Froggee answers with a shout
As he sees us go about,
Which was grateful of the poor Mounseer,
D'ye see?
Which was grateful of the poor Mounseer!
And I'll wager in their joy they kissed each other's cheek
(Which is what them furriners do),
And they blessed their lucky stars
We were hardy British tars
Who had pity on a poor Parly-voo,
D'ye see?
Who had pity on a poor Parly-voo!

9

BRIDESMAIDS	Who had pity on a poor Parly-voo, D'ye see?
	Who had pity on a poor Parly-voo!

Music No. 6a   HORNPIPE

[*Exeunt* CHORUS. *Enter* ROBIN.

ROBIN	Richard!
RICHARD	Robin!
ROBIN	My beloved foster-brother, and very dearest friend, welcome home again after ten long years at sea! It is such deeds as yours that cause our flag to be loved and dreaded throughout the civilized world!
RICHARD	Why, lord love ye, Rob., that's but a trifle to what we *have* done in the way of sparing life! I believe I may say, without exaggeration, that the marciful little Tom-Tit has spared more French frigates than any craft afloat! But 'taint for a British seaman to brag, so I'll just stow my jawin' tackle and belay. (ROBIN *sighs*) But 'vast heavin', messmate, what's brought *you* all a-cockbill?
ROBIN	Alas, Dick, I love Rose Maybud, and love in vain!
RICHARD	*You* love in vain? Come, that's too good! Why you're a fine strapping muscular young fellow—tall and strong as a to'-gall'n-m'st—taut as a fore-stay—aye, and a barrowknight to boot, if all had their rights!
ROBIN	Hush, Richard—not a word about my true rank, which none here suspect. Yes, I know well enough that few men are better calculated to win a woman's heart than I. I'm a fine fellow, Dick, and worthy any woman's love—happy the girl who gets me, say I. But I'm timid, Dick; shy—nervous—modest—retiring—diffident—and I cannot tell her, Dick, I cannot tell her! Ah, you've no idea what a poor opinion I have of myself, and how little I deserve it.
RICHARD	Robin, do you call to mind how, years ago, we swore that, come what might, we would always act upon our hearts' dictates?
ROBIN	Aye, Dick, and I've always kept that oath. In doubt, difficulty and danger, I've always asked my heart what I should do, and it has never failed me.
RICHARD	Right! Let your heart be your compass, with a clear conscience for your binnacle light, and you'll sail ten knots on a bowline, clear of shoals, rocks and quicksands! Well, now, what does my heart say in this here difficult situation? Why it says "Dick," it says—(it calls me "Dick" acos it's known me from a babby)—"Dick," it says, "*you* ain't shy—*you* ain't modest—speak you up for him as is!" Robin, my lad, just you lay me alongside, and when she's becalmed under my lee, I'll spin her a yarn that shall sarve to fish you two together for life!
ROBIN	Will you do this thing for me? Can you, do you think? Yes (*feeling his pulse*). There's no false modesty about *you*. Your—what I would call

ROBIN (Contd.)	bumptious self-assertiveness (I mean the expression in its complimentary sense), has already made you a bos'n's mate, and it will make an admiral of you in time, if you work it properly, you dear, incompetent old imposter! My dear fellow, I'd give my right arm for one tenth of your modest assurance!
Music No. 7.	SONG—(Robin, with Richard) "My boy, you may take it from me"

SONG—ROBIN

ROBIN	My boy, you may take it from me, That of all the afflictions accurst With which a man's saddled And hampered and addled, A diffident nature's the worst. Though clever as clever can be— A Crichton of early romance— You must stir it and stump it, And blow your own trumpet, Or, trust me, you haven't a chance, If you wish in the world to advance, Your merits you're bound to enhance, Your must stir it and stump it, And blow your own trumpet, Or, trust me, you haven't a chance! Now take, for example, *my* case: I've a bright intellectual brain— In all London city There's no one so witty— I've thought so again and again. I've a highly intelligent face— My features cannot be denied— But, whatever I try, sir, I fail in—and why, sir? I'm modesty personified! If you wish in the world to advance, Your merits you're bound to enhance, You must stir it and stump it, And blow your own trumpet, Or, trust me, you haven't a chance. As a poet, I'm tender and quaint— I've passion and fervour and grace— From Ovid and Horace To Swinburne and Morris, They all of them take a back place. Then I sing and I play and I paint: Though none are accomplished as I, To say so were treason: You ask me the reason? I'm diffident, modest and shy! If you wish in the world to advance, Your merits you're bound to enhance,

ROBIN (Contd.)	You must stir it and stump it, And blow your own trumpet, Or, trust me, you haven't a chance.
ROBIN and RICHARD	If you wish in the world to advance, Your merits you're bound to enhance, You must stir it and stump it, And blow your own trumpet, Or, trust me, you haven't a chance!

(Exit ROBIN)

RICHARD	(*looking after him*). Ah, it's a thousand pities he's such a poor opinion of himself, for a finer fellow don't walk! Well, I'll do my best for him. "Plead for him as though it was for your own father"—that's what my heart's a-remarkin' to me just now. But here she comes! Steady! Steady it is! By the Port Admiral, but she's a tight little craft! Come, come, she's not for you, Dick, and yet—she's fit to marry Lord Nelson! By the Flag of Old England, I can't look at her unmoved.

(Enter ROSE—he is much struck by her)

ROSE	Sir, you are agitated—
RICHARD	Aye, aye, my lass, well said! I am agitated, true enough!—took flat aback, my girl, but 'tis naught—'twill pass. (*Aside*). This here heart of mine's a-dictatin' to me like anythink. Question is, have I a right to disregard its promptings?
ROSE	Can I do aught to relieve thine anguish, for it seemeth to me that thou art in sore trouble? This apple—(*offering a damaged apple*).
RICHARD	(*looking at it and returning it*). No, my lass, 'taint that: I'm—I'm took flat aback—I never see anything like you in all my born days. Parbuckle me, if you ain't the loveliest gal I've ever set eyes on. There—I can't say fairer than that, can I?
ROSE	No. (*Aside*) The question is, Is it meet that an utter stranger should thus express himself? (*Refers to book*). Yes,—"Always speak the truth."
RICHARD	I'd no thoughts of sayin' this here to you on my own account, for, truth to tell, I was chartered by another; but when I see you my heart it up and it says, says it, "This is the very lass for *you*, Dick"—"speak up to her, Dick," it says—(it calls me Dick acos we was at school together)—"tell her all, Dick," it says, "never sail under false colours— it's mean!" *That's* what my heart tells me to say, and in my rough, common-sailor fashion, I've said it, and I'm a-waiting for your reply. I'm a-tremblin', miss. Lookye here—(*holding out his hand*). That's narvousness!
ROSE	(*aside*). Now, how should a maiden deal with such an one? (*Consults book*) "Keep no one in unnecessary suspense." (*Aloud*) Behold, I will not keep you in unnecessary suspense. (*Refers to book*) "In accepting

ROSE (Contd.)	an offer of marriage, do so with apparent hesitation." (*Aloud*) I take you, but with a certain show of reluetance. (*Refers to book*) "Avoid any appearance of eagerness." (*Aloud*). Though you will bear in mind that I am far from anxious to do so. *(Refers to book)* "A little show of emotion will not be misplaced!" (*Aloud*) Pardon this tear! (*Wipes her eye.*)
RICHARD	Rose, you've made me the happiest blue-jacket in England! I wouldn't change places with the Admiral of the Fleet, no matter who he's a-huggin' of at this present moment! But, axin' your pardon, miss (*wiping his lips with his hand*), might I be permitted to salute the flag I'm a-goin' to sail under?
ROSE	(*Referring to book*) "An engaged young lady should not permit too many familiarities." (*Aloud*) Once! (*Richard kisses her*).
Music No. 8	DUET—(Rose and Richard) "The battle's roar is over"
RICHARD	The battle's roar is over, O my love! Embrace thy tender lover, O my love! From tempest's welter, From war's alarms, O give me shelter Within those arms, O give me shelter Within those arms! Thy smile alluring All heartache curing, Gives peace enduring, O my love! O my love!
ROSE	If heart both true and tender, O my love! A life-love can engender, O my love! A truce to sighing, And tears of brine, For joy undying Shall aye be mine, For joy undying Shall aye be mine,

ROSE	**RICHARD**
And thou	
	And thou and I,
and I, love,	love,
Shall live	
	Shall live and die,
and die, love,	love,

	ROSE (Contd.)	**RICHARD (Contd.)**
	Without a sigh, love,	Without a sigh, love,
	Without a sigh	Without a sigh,
		My own,
	My	
	own, my	my
	love!	love!
TOGETHER	And thou and I, love,	
	Shall live and die, love,	
	Without a sigh, love,	
	My own, my love!	

(Enter ROBIN, with CHORUS OF BRIDESMAIDS)

Music No. 9   ENTRANCE OF BRIDESMAIDS

"If well his suit has sped"

BRIDESMAIDS
If well his suit has sped,
Oh, may they soon be wed!
Oh, tell us, tell us, pray,
What doth the maiden say?
In singing are we justified,
In singing are we justified,
Hail the Bridegroom—hail the Bride!
Let the nuptial knot be tied:
In fair phrases
Hymn their praises,
Hail the Bridegroom—hail the Bride?

ROBIN   Well—what news? Have you spoken to her?

RICHARD   Aye, my lad, I have—so to speak—spoke her.

ROBIN   And she refuses?

RICHARD   Why, no, I can't truly say she do.

ROBIN   (*Embraces her*) Then she accepts! My darling!

BRIDESMAIDS
Hail the Bridegroom—hail the Bride!
When the nuptial knot is tied,
In fair phrases
Hymn their praises,
Hail the Bridegroom—hail the Bride!

ROSE   (*aside, referring to her book*). Now, what should a maiden do when she is embraced by the wrong gentleman?

RICHARD   Belay, my lad, belay. You don't understand.

ROSE   Oh, sir, belay, I beseech you!

RICHARD   You see, it's like this: she accepts—but it's *me!*

ROBIN   You!   [RICHARD *embraces* ROSE

BRIDESMAIDS	Hail the Bridegroom—hail the Bride! When the nuptial knot is tied—
ROBIN	(*interrupting angrily*). Hold your tongues, will you! Now then, what does this mean?
RICHARD	My poor lad, my heart grieves for thee, but it's like this: the moment I see her, and just as I was a-goin' to mention your name, my heart it up and it says, says it—"Dick, you've fell in love with her yourself," it says; "be honest and sailor-like—don't skulk under false colours—speak up," it says, "take her, you dog, and with her my blessin,!"
BRIDESMAIDS	Hail the Bridegroom—hail the Bride!—
ROBIN	Will you be quiet! Go away! (*Chorus make faces at him and exeunt.*) Vulgar girls!
RICHARD	What could I do? I'm bound to obey my heart's dictates.
ROBIN	Of course—no doubt. It's quite right—I don't mind—that is, not particularly—only it's—it *is* disappointing, you know
ROSE	(*to* ROBIN). Oh, but, sir, I knew not that thou did'st seek me in wedlock, or in very truth I should not have hearkened unto this man, for behold, he is but a lowly mariner, and very poor withal, whereas thou art a tiller of the land, and thou hast fat oxen, and many sheep and swine, a considerable dairy farm and much corn and oil!
RICHARD	That's true, my lass, but it's done now, ain't it, Rob?
ROSE	Still, it may be that I should not be happy in thy love. I am passing young and little able to judge. Moreover, as to thy character I know naught!
ROBIN	Nay, Rose, I'll answer for that. Dick has won thy love fairly. Broken-hearted as I am, I'll stand up for Dick through thick and thin!
RICHARD	(*with emotion*). Thankye, messmate! that's well said. That's spoken honest, Thankye, Rob! (*Grasps his hand*).
ROSE	Yet methinks I have heard that sailors are but worldly men, and little prone to lead serious and thoughtful lives!
ROBIN	And what then? Admit that Dick is *not* a steady character, and that when he's excited he uses language that would make your hair curl. Grant that—he does. It's the truth, and I'm not going to deny it. But look at his *good* qualities. He's as nimble as a pony, and his hornpipe is the talk of the fleet!
RICHARD	Thankye, Rob! That's well spoken. Thankye, Rob!
ROSE	But it maybe that he drinketh strong waters which do bemuse a man, and make him even as the wild beasts of the desert!

15

ROBIN	Well, suppose he does, and I don't say he don't, for rum's his bane, and ever has been. He *does* drink—I won't deny it. But what of that? Look at his arms—tattooed to the shoulder! (RICHARD *rolls up his sleeves*) No, no—I won't hear a word against Dick!
ROSE	But they say that mariners are but rarely true to those whom they profess to love!
ROBIN	Granted—granted—and I don't say that Dick isn't as bad as any of 'em. (RICHARD *chuckles*.) You are, you know you are, you dog! a devil of a fellow—a regular out-and-out Lothario! But what then? You can't have everything, and a better hand at turning-in a dead-eye don't walk a deck! And what an accomplishment *that* is in a family man! No, no—not a word against Dick. I'll stick up for him through thick and thin!
RICHARD	Thankye, Rob, thankye. You're a true friend. I've acted accordin' to my heart's dictates, and such orders as them no man should disobey.
Music No. 10	TRIO—(Rose, Richard, and Robin)

"In sailing o'er life's ocean wide"

ROSE	**RICHARD & ROBIN**
In sailing o'er life's ocean wide Your heart should be	In sailing o'er life's ocean wide Your heart should be
your only guide; With summer sea and fav'ring wind Yourself in port you'll find.	your only guide; With summer sea and fav'ring wind Yourself in port you'll surely find.

SOLO—RICHARD

My heart says, "To this maiden strike—
She's captur'd you.
She's just the sort of girl you like—
You know you do.
If other man her heart should gain,
I shall resign."
That's what it says to me quite plain,
This heart of mine! This heart of mine!

SOLO—ROBIN

My heart says, "You've a prosperous lot,
With acres wide.
You mean to settle all you've got
Upon your bride.
It don't pretend to shape my acts
By word or sign;
It merely states these simple facts
This heart of mine! This heart of mine!

SOLO—ROSE

Ten minutes since my heart said "white"—
It now says "black".
It then said "left"—it now says "right"—
Hearts often tack.
I must obey its latest strain—
You tell me so.   (*To* RICHARD)
But should it change its mind again,
I'll let you know, I'll let you know.
(*Turning from* RICHARD *to* ROBIN, *who embraces her*)

ROSE	RICHARD & ROBIN
In sailing o'er life's ocean wide No doubt	In sailing o'er life's ocean wide No doubt the heart
the heart should be your guide, But it is awkward when you find A heart, a heart that does not know its mind, A heart, --------- -------------- A heart, a heart that does	should be your guide, But it is awkward when you find A heart, a heart that does not know its mind, A heart that does not know its mind, A heart, a heart
not know its mind!	that does not know its mind!

TOGETHER A heart, a heart, that does not know its mind!

(Exeunt ROBIN with ROSE L. and RICHARD R.)

(Enter MAD MARGARET. She is wildly dressed in picturesque tatters, and is an obvious caricature of theatrical madness.)

Music No. 11   RECIT. and ARIA—(Margaret)

"Cheerily carols the lark"

SCENA—MARGARET

Cheerily carols the lark
Over the cot.

Merrily whistles the clerk
Scratching a blot.
But the lark
And the clerk,
I remark,
Comfort me not!
Over the ripening peach
Buzzes the bee.
Splash on the billowy beach
Tumbles the sea.
But the peach
And the beach
They are each
Nothing to me!
And why?
Who am I?
Daft Madge! Crazy Meg.
Mad Margaret! Poor Peg!
He! he! he! (*chuckling*)
Mad, I?
Yes, very!
But why?
Mystery!
Don't call!
Whisht! whisht!
No crime—
'Tis only
That I'm
Love—lonely!
That's all!
Whisht! wisht!

BALLAD.

To a garden full of posies
Cometh one to gather flowers,
And he wanders through its bowers
Toying with the wanton roses, the wanton roses,
Who, uprising from their beds,
Hold on high their shameless heads
With their pretty lips a-pouting,
With their pretty lips a-pouting,
Never doubting, never doubting
That for Cytherean posies
He would gather aught but roses!

In a nest of weeds and nettles,
Lay a violet, half hidden,
Hoping that his glance unbidden
Yet might fall upon her petals, upon her petals,
Though she lived alone, apart,
Hope lay nestling at her heart,
But, alas, the cruel awaking,
But, alas, the cruel awaking

But, alas, the cruel awaking
Set her little heart a-breaking,
For he gather'd for his posies
Only roses, only roses!

(*Bursts into tears*)

Enter ROSE.

ROSE	A maiden, and in tears? Can I do aught to soften thy sorrow? This apple—(*offering apple*).
MARGARET	((*Examines it and rejects it*) No! (*mysteriously*). Tell me, are you mad?
ROSE	I? No! That is, I think not.
MARGARET	That's well! Then you don't love Sir Despard Murgatroyd? All mad girls love him. *I* love him. I'm poor Mad Margaret—Crazy Meg—Poor Peg! He! he! he! he! (*chuckling*)
ROSE	Thou lovest the bad Baronet of Ruddigore? Oh, horrible—too horrible!

MARGARET	You pity me? Then be my mother! The squirrel had a mother, but she drank and the squirrel fled! Hush! They sing a brave song in our parts—it runs somewhat thus:—(*Sings*)
	   "The cat and the dog and the little puppee
	     Sat down in a—down in a—in a"
	I forget what they sat down in, but so the song goes! Listen—I've come to pinch her!

ROSE	Mercy, whom!
MARGARET	You mean "who"
ROSE	Nay! it is the accusative after the verb.
MARGARET	True. (*Whispers melodramatically*) I have come to pinch Rose Maybud!
ROSE	(*Aside, alarmed*) Rose Maybud!
MARGARET	Aye! I love him—he loved me once. But that's all gone, Fisht! He gave me an Italian glance—thus—(*business*)—and made me his. He will give *her* an Italian glance, and make *her* his. But it shall not be, for I'll stamp on her—stamp on her—stamp on her! Did you ever kill anybody! No? Why not? Listen—I killed a fly this morning! It buzzed, and I wouldn't have it. So it died—pop! So shall she!
ROSE	But behold, *I* am Rose Maybud, and I would fain not die "pop".
MARGARET	You are Rose Maybud!
ROSE	Yes, sweet Rose Maybud!

MARGARET	Strange! They told me she was beautiful! And *he* loves *you!* No, no! If I thought that, I would treat you as the auctioneer and land-agent treated the lady-bird—I would rend you asunder!
ROSE	Nay, be pacified, for behold I am pledged to another, and lo, we are to be wedded this very day!
MARGARET	Swear me that! Come to a Commissioner and let me have it on affidavit! *I* once made an affidavit—but it died—it died—it died! ˥ut see, they come—Sir Despard and his evil crew! Hide, hide—they are all mad—quite mad!
ROSE	What makes you think that?
MARGARET	Hush! They sing choruses in public. That's mad enough, I think! Go—hide away, or they will seize you. Hush! Quite softly—quite, quite softly!

[Exeunt together, on tiptoe.

(Enter CHORUS OF BUCKS AND BLADES, heralded by CHORUS OF BRIDESMAIDS.)

Music No. 12.	**CHORUS**
	"Welcome, gentry"
BRIDESMAIDS	Welcome, gentry, For your entry, Sets out tender hearts a-beating, Men of station, Admiration Prompts this unaffected greeting. Hearty greeting, hearty greeting offer we!
BUCKS & BLADES	When thoroughly tired Of being admired By ladies of gentle degree—degree, With flattery sated, High-flown and inflated, Away from the city we flee—we flee! From charms intramural To prettiness rural The sudden transition Is simply Elysian, Come, Amaryllis, Come, Chloe and Phyllis, Your slaves, for the moment, are we! Your slaves, for the moment, your slaves are we!
BRIDESMAIDS	The sons of the tillage Who dwell in this village Are people of lowly degree—degree.

BRIDESMAIDS
(Contd.)

Though honest and active
They're most unattractive
And awkward as awkward can be—can be.
They're clumsy clodhoppers
With axes and choppers,
And shepherds and ploughmen
And drovers and cowmen
Hedgers and reapers
And carters and keepers,
But never a lover for me!
But never a lover for me!

GIRLS

Hearty greet-

ing
offer we, offer we! So

wel-
come,
gen-
try,
For
your
en-
try
Sets
our
ten-
der
hearts
a-
beat-
ing.
Men
of
sta-
tion,
Ad-
mi-
ra-
tion
Prompts
this
un-
af-
fect-
ed
greeting

Hearty
greeting
Hearty
greeting offer we!

MEN

Then come, Amaryllis,

Come,
Chloe and Phyllis

When
thoroughly
tired Of
being ad-
mired By
ladies of
gentle de-
gree—de-
green, With
flattery
sated, High-
flown and in-
flated, A-
way from the city
we
flee—we
flee! From
charms intra-
mural to
prettiness
rural The
sudden trans-
ition Is
simply E-
lysian,
Come, Ama-
ryllis, Come,
Chloe and
Phyllis, Your
slaves, for the
moment, are
we,
Your
slaves
for the
mo-
ment, your slaves are we!

GIRLS (Contd.)	**MEN** (Contd.)
welcome!	welcome!
Welcome, welcome,	Welcome, welcome,
welcome, welcome we!	welcome, welcome we!

(Enter SIR DESPARD MURGATROYD)

Music No. 13.	SONG—(Sir Despard) and CHORUS
	"Oh, why am I moody and sad?"
SIR DESPARD	Oh why am I moody and sad?
CHORUS	Can't guess!
SIR DESPARD	And why am I guiltily mad?
CHORUS	Confess!
SIR DESPARD	Because I am thoroughly bad!
CHORUS	Oh yes—
SIR DESPARD	You'll see it at once in my face. Oh why am I husky and hoarse?
CHORUS	Ah, why?
SIR DESPARD	It's the workings of conscience, of course.
CHORUS	Fie, fie!
SIR DESPARD	And huskiness stands for remorse,
CHORUS	Oh my!
SIR DESPARD	At least it does so in my case!
SIR DESPARD	When in crime one is fully employed—
CHORUS	Like you—
SIR DESPARD	Your expression gets warped and destroyed
CHORUS	It do.
SIR DESPARD	It's a penalty none can avoid;
CHORUS	How true!
SIR DESPARD	I once was a nice-looking youth; But like stone from a strong catapult—
CHORUS	(*explaining to each other*). A trice—
SIR DESPARD	I rushed at my terrible cult—

CHORUS	(*explaining to each other*). That's vice—
SIR DESPARD	Observe the unpleasant result!
CHORUS	Not nice.
SIR DESPARD	Indeed I am telling the truth!
SIR DESPARD	Oh innocents, happy though poor!
CHORUS	That's we—
SIR DESPARD	If I had been virtuous, I'm sure—
CHORUS	Like me—
SIR DESPARD	I should be as nice-looking as you're!
CHORUS	May be.
SIR DESPARD	You are very nice-looking indeed! Oh innocents, listen in time—
CHORUS	We *doe*,
SIR DESPARD	Avoid an existence of crime—
CHORUS	Just so—
SIR DESPARD	Or you'll be as ugly as I'm
CHORUS	(*loudly*). No! No!
SIR DESPARD	And now, if you please, we'll proceed.

(*All the girls express their horror of* SIR DESPARD. *As he approaches them they fly from him, terror-stricken, leaving him alone on the stage.*)

SIR DESPARD	Poor children, how they loathe me—me whose hands are certainly steeped in infamy, but whose heart is as the heart of a little child! But what *is* a poor baronet to do, when a whole picture-gallery of ancestors step down from their frames and threaten him with an excruciating death if he hesitate to commit his daily crime? But ha! ha! I am even with them! (*Mysteriously*) I get my crime over the first thing in the morning and then, ha! ha! for the rest of the day I do good—I do good—I do good! (*Melodramatically*). Two days since, I stole a child and built an orphan asylum. Yesterday I robbed a bank and endowed a bishopric. To-day I carry off Rose Maybud, and atone with a cathedral! This is what it is to be the sport and toy of a Picture Gallery! But I will be bitterly revenged upon them! I will give them all to the Nation, and nobody shall ever look upon their faces again!

Enter RICHARD

RICHARD	Ax your honour's pardon, but—
SIR DESPARD	Ha! observed! And by a mariner! What would you with me, fellow?
RICHARD	Your honour, I'm a poor man-o'-war's man, becalmed in the doldrums—
SIR DESPARD	I don't know them.
RICHARD	And I make bold to ax your honour's advice. Does your honour know what it is to have a heart?
SIR DESPARD	My honour knows what it is to have a complete apparatus for conducting the circulation of the blood through the veins and arteries of the human body.
RICHARD	Aye, but has your honour a heart that ups and looks you in the face, and gives you quarter-deck orders that it's life and death to disobey?
SIR DESPARD	I have not a heart of that description, but I have a Picture Gallery that presumes to take that liberty
RICHARD	Well, your honour, it's like this—Your honour had an elder brother—
SIR DESPARD	It had.
RICHARD	Who should have inherited your title, and with it its cuss.
SIR DESPARD	Aye, but he died. Oh, Ruthven!—
RICHARD	He didn't.
SIR DESPARD	He did *not?*
RICHARD	He didn't. On the contrary, he lives in this here very village, under the name of Robin Oakapple, and he's a-going to marry Rose Maybud this very day.
SIR DESPARD	Ruthven alive, and going to marry Rose Maybud! Can this be possible?
RICHARD	Now the question I was going to ask your honour is—ought I to tell your honour this?
SIR DESPARD	I don't know. It's a delicate point. I think you ought. Mind, I'm not sure, but I think so.
RICHARD	That's what my heart says. It says, "Dick," it says, (it calls me Dick acos it's entitled to take that liberty). "That there young gal would recoil from him if she knowed what he really were. Ought you to stand off and on, and let this young gal take this false step and never fire a shot across her bows to bring her to? No, it says, "you did *not* ought." And I won't ought, accordin'.

24

SIR DESPARD	Then you really feel yourself at liberty to tell me that my elder brother lives—that I may charge him with his cruel deceit, and transfer to his shoulders the hideous thraldom under which I have laboured for so many years! Free—free at last! Free to live a blameless life, and to die beloved and regretted by all who knew me!
Music No. 14.	DUET—(Richard and Sir Despard) "You understand? I think I do"
RICHARD	You understand?
SIR DESPARD	I think I do, With vigour unshaken This step shall be taken, It's neatly plann'd.
RICHARD	I think so too; I'll readily bet it You'll never regret it!
BOTH	For duty, duty must be done; The rule applies to ev'ry one, And painful though that duty be, To shirk the task were fiddle-de-dee, To shirk the task were fiddle-de-dee, To shirk the task, To shirk the task were fiddle-de, fiddle-de, fiddle-de, fiddle-de, fiddle-de, fiddle-de, fiddle-de-dee!
SIR DESPARD	The bridegroom comes—
RICHARD	Likewise the bride— The maidens are very Elated and merry; They are her chums.
SIR DESPARD	To lash their pride, Were almost a pity, The pretty committee!
BOTH	But duty, duty must be done; The rule applies to ev'ry one, And painful though that duty be, To shirk the task were fiddle-de-dee, To shirk the task were fiddle-de-dee, To shirk the task, To shirk the task were fiddle-de, fiddle-de, fiddle-de, fiddle-de, fiddle-de, fiddle-de, fiddle-de-dee!

(Exeunt RICHARD and SIR DESPARD)

(Enter CHORUS of BRIDESMAIDS and BUCKS)

Music No. 15. FINALE—ACT I

"Hail the bride"

GIRLS **CHORUS OF BRIDESMAIDS**
Hail the bride of seventeen summers:
In fair phrases
Hymn her praises;
Lift your song on high, all comers,
She rejoices
In your voices
Smiling summer beams upon her,
Shedding ev'ry blessing on her:
Maidens, greet her—
Kindly treat her—
You may all be brides some day!

CHORUS OF BUCKS

Hail the bridegroom who advances,
Agitated,
Yet elated.
He's in easy circumstances,
Young and lusty,
True and trusty.

GIRLS & MEN Smiling summer beams upon her,
Shedding ev'ry blessing on her;
Maidens greet her—
Kindly treat her—
You may all, may all be brides some day!

(Enter ROBIN, attended by RICHARD and OLD
ADAM, meeting ROSE, attended by ZORAH and
DAME HANNAH. ROSE and ROBIN embrace.)

MADRIGAL.

ROSE When the buds are blossoming,
Smiling welcome to the spring,
Lovers choose a wedding day
Life is love in merry May,
Life is love, life is love, in merry May!

ROSE	HANNAH	RICHARD	ADAM	CHORUS.SOPRANOS
				Spring is green
Fa la la la la la la la!	Fa la la la la la la la!	Fa la la la la!	Fa la la la la!	
				Summer's rose
Fa la la la la la la la! It is sad when summer goes, Fa la la la la! Fa la!	Fa la la la la la la la! It is sad when summer goes, Fa la la la la! Fa la la!	Fa la la la la! It is sad when summer goes, Fa la! Fa la la la la la!	Fa la la la la! It is sad when summer goes, Fa la! Fa la la la la la!	
				CHORUS.TENORS
				Autumn's gold,
	Fa la la la la la la la!	Fa la la la la la la la!	Fa la la la la!	
				Winter's grey,
Fa la la la la la la la!	Fa la la la la!	Fa la la la la!	Fa la la la la!	

ROSE, HANNAH, ADAM
Winter still is far away, far away—
Fa la la la la la!

RICHARD
Winter still is far away, far away—
Fa la la la la!
Fa la la la la la

CHORUS SOPRANOS	CONTRALTOS	TENORS	BASSES
Leaves in autumn fade and fall, Winter is the end of all.	Leaves in autumn fade and fall, Winter is the end of all.	Leaves in autumn fade and fall, Winter is the end of all.	Leaves in autumn fade and fall, Winter is the end of all. Fa la la!
Fa la la la la la la, - - - la la la la la la la! Fa la - - - la la la la la! Fa la la la la la la la la!	Spring and summer teem with glee: Spring and summer then, for me! Fa la la la la la la la la! Fa la! Fa - - - la la la la! Fa la la la la la la la!	Spring and summer teem with glee: Spring and summer, then, for me! ---Fa la la la la la la la la! Fa la la la la! Fa la la la la la la la!	Spring and summer teem with glee: Spring and summer, then, for me! - - - Fa la la! Fa la la la la la! Fa la la la la la la la!

HANNAH

In the springtime seed is sown:
In the summer grass is mown:
In the autumn you may reap:
Winter is the time for sleep,
Winter is the time for sleep.

ROSE	HANNAH	RICHARD	ADAM	CHORUS.SOPRANOS
				Spring is hope
Fa la la la la la la la!	Fa la la la la la la la!	Fa la la la la la!	Fa la la la la!	
				Summer's joy
Fa la la la la la la la! Spring and summer never cloy, Fa la - - la la la la! Fa la!	Fa la la la la la la la! Spring and summer never cloy, Fa - - - la la la la! Fa la la!	Fa la la la la! Spring and summer never cloy, Fa la! Fa la la - - la la la la!	Fa la la la la! Spring and summer never cloy, Fa la! Fa la la la la la!	

CHORUS, TENORS
Autumn, toil

ROSE	HANNAH	RICHARD	ADAM
	Fa la la la la la la la!	Fa la la la la la la la!	Fa la la la la!

Winter, rest

| Fa la la la la la la la! | Fa la la la la! | Fa la la la la! | Fa la la la la! |

ROSE, HANNAH, ADAM
Winter, after all, is best, after all,
Fa la la la la!

RICHARD
Winter, after all, is best, after all,
Fa la la la la la!
Fa la la la la la

CHORUS

SOPRANOS	CONTRALTOS	TENORS	BASSES
Spring and summer pleasure you, Autumn, aye, and winter too	Spring and summer pleasure you, Autumn, aye, and winter too	Spring and summer pleasure you, Autumn, aye, and winter too	Spring and summer pleasure you, Autumn, aye, and winter too Fa la la!
Fa la la la la la la la - - la la la la la la la	Ev'ry season has its cheer, Life is lovely all the year! Fa la la la la la la la la la	Ev'ry season has its cheer Life is lovely all the year - - - Fa la la la la la	Ev'ry season has its cheer, Life is lovely all the year - - - Fa

28

SOPRANOS (Contd.)	CONTRALTOS (Contd.)	TENORS (Contd.)	BASSES (Contd.)
la! Fa	la! Fa	la la la la	la
la	la! Fa	la! Fa	la! Fa
- - - la la la	- - - la	la	la la
la la	la la	la la	la la
la! Fa	la! Fa	la! Fa	la! Fa
la la la la	la la	la la	la la
la la la la la!	la la la la la!	la la la la la!	la la la la la!

GAVOTTE.

After GAVOTTE, enter SIR DESPARD

SIR DESPARD

Hold, bride and bridegroom, ere you wed each other,
I claim young Robin as my elder brother!
His rightful title I have long enjoyed:
I claim him as Sir Ruthven Murgatroyd!

ALL

O Wonder!

ROSE

(*Wildly*) Deny the falsehood, Robin, as you should!
It is a plot!

ROBIN

I would, if conscientiously I could,
But I cannot!

ALL

Ah, base one! Ah, base one!

SOLO—Robin

As pure and blameless peasant,
I cannot, I regret,
Deny a truth unpleasant,
I am that Baronet!

ALL

He is that Baronet!

ROBIN

But when completely rated
Bad baronet am I,
That I am what he's stated
I'll recklessly deny!

ALL

He'll recklessly deny!

ROBIN

When I'm a bad Bart. I will tell taradiddles!

ALL

He'll tell taradiddles when he's a bad Bart.

ROBIN

I'll play a bad part on the falsest of fiddles.

ALL

On very false fiddles he'll play a bad part!

ROBIN

But until that takes place I must be conscientious—

ALL

He'll be conscientious until that takes place.

ROBIN Then adieu with good grace to my morals sententious!

ALL To morals sententious adieu with good grace!
Adieu with good grace to his morals, his morals sententious!

ROBIN	**CHORUS**
When I'm a bad Bart. I will tell taradiddles!	When he's a bad Bart. He will tell taradiddles!
On very false fiddles I'll play a bad part!	On very false fiddles He'll play a bad part!
I'll play a bad part on the falsest of fiddles,	He'll play a bad part on the falsest of fiddles,
And tell taradiddles when I'm a bad Bart!	And tell taradiddles when he's a bad Bart!

CHORUS When he's a bad Bart. he will tell taradiddles!
On very false fiddles he'll play a bad part,
He'll play a bad part on the falsest of fiddles,
And tell taradiddles When he's a bad Bart.,

GIRLS	**MEN**
A bad	When he's a bad Bart. he will
Bart.!	tell taradiddles,
When he's a bad Bart. he will tell taradiddles,	When he's a bad Bart. he will tell taradiddles,
A bad	He'll play a bad part on the
Bart!	falsest of fiddles,
On very false fiddles, on very false fiddles	On very false fiddles, on very false fiddles
he'll play a bad part!	he'll play a bad part!

ZORAH Who is the wretch who hath betray'd thee?
Let him stand forth!

RICHARD (*coming forward*) 'Twas I!

ALL Die, traitor!

RICHARD Hold, my conscience made me!
Withhold your wrath!

SOLO—Richard.

Within this breast there beats a heart
Whose voice can't be gainsaid.
It bade me thy true rank impart,
And I at once obey'd.
I knew 'twould blight thy budding fate—
I knew 'twould cause thee anguish great—
But did I therefore hesitate?
No! I at once obey'd!

ALL Acclaim him who, when his true heart
Bade him young Robin's rank impart,
Immediately obey'd!

SOLO—Rose (addressing Robin)

Farewell!
Thou had'st my heart—

SOLO—Rose (addressing Robin).

'Twas quickly won!
But now we part—
Thy face I shun!
Farewell!
Go, bend the knee
At Vice's shrine,
Of life with me
All hope resign.
Farewell! farewell! Farewell!
(*To Sir Despard*) Take me—I am thy bride!

BRIDESMAIDS   Hail the Bridegroom—hail the Bride!
When the nuptial knot is tied;
Every day will bring some joy
That can never, never cloy!

Enter MARGARET, who listens.

SIR DESPARD   Excuse me, I'm a virtuous person now—

ROSE   That's why I wed you!

SIR DESPARD   And I to Margaret must keep my vow!

MARGARET   Have I misread you?
Oh joy! with newly kindled rapture warm'd,
I kneel before you!   (*Kneels*)

SIR DESPARD   I once disliked you; now that I've reformed,
How I adore you!   (*They embrace*)

BRIDESMAIDS   Hail the Bridegroom—hail the Bride!
When the nuptial knot is tied;
Ev'ry day will bring some joy
That can never, never cloy!

ROSE   Richard, of him I love bereft,
Through thy design,
Thou art the only one that's left,
So I am thine!   (*They embrace*)

BRIDESMAIDS   Hail the Bridegroom—hail the Bride!
Hail the Bridegroom—hail the Bride!

DUET—ROSE and RICHARD

BOTH   Oh, happy the lily
When kiss'd by the bee;
And sipping tranquilly,
Quite happy is he;
And happy the filly
That neighs in her pride;

31

ROSE

But
happier than
any
A
pound
to a
penny,
A
lo-
ver is,
when he
Embraces his bride!

RICHARD

But
happier than
a-
ny
A
pound to a
pen-
ny,
A
lover is,
when
he
Embraces his bride!

DUET—SIR DESPARD and MARGARET

BOTH

Oh, happy the flowers
That blossom in June,
And happy the bowers,
That gain by the boon,
But happier by hours
The man of descent,

MARGARET

Who,
folly re-
gretting,
Is
bent
on for-
getting
His
bad
baron-
etting,
And means to repent!

SIR DESPARD

Who,
folly re-
gret-
ting,
Is
bent on for-
get-
ting
His
bad baron-
et-
ting,
And means to repent!

TRIO—HANNAH, ADAM, and ZORAH.

ALL THREE

Oh, happy the blossom
That blooms on the lea,
Likewise the opossum
That sits on a tree,
When you come across 'em,
They cannot compare

HANNAH
With
those who are
tread-
ing

ZORAH & ADAM

With
those who are
treading

HANNAH	ZORAH & ADAM
The	The
dance at a	dance
wed-	at a
ding,	wedding,
While	While
people are	peo-
spread-	ple are
ing	spreading
The best of good fare!	The best of good fare!

SOLO—ROBIN

Oh, wretched the debtor
Who's signing a deed!
And wretched the letter
That no one can read!
But very much better
Their lot it must be
Than that of the person
I'm making this verse on,
Whose head there's a curse on—
Alluding to me!

CHORUS

Oh, happy the lily
When kiss'd by the bee;
And, sipping tranquilly,
Quite happy is he;
And happy the filly
That neighs in her pride;

GIRLS AND BASSES	TENORS
	But
But	happier than
happier than	a-
any	ny
A	A
pound	pound to a
to a	pen-
penny,	ny,
A	A
lo-	lover is,
ver is,	when
when he	he
Embraces his bride!	Embraces his bride!

ALL CHORUS   Embraces his bride!
Embraces his bride!

DANCE

END OF ACT I.

33

ACT II

(SCENE: *Picture Gallery in Ruddigore Castle. The walls are covered with full length portraits of the Baronets of Ruddigore from the time of* JAMES I—*the first being that of* SIR RUPERT, *alluded to in the legend; the last, that of the last deceased Baronet,* SIR RODERIC.)

Enter ROBIN and ADAM melodramatically. They are greatly altered in appearance, SIR RUTHVEN wearing the haggard aspect of a guilty roué; ADAM, that of the wicked steward to such a man.

Music No. 1.   DUET—SIR RUTHVEN and ADAM.

"I once was as meek"

SIR RUTHVEN

I once was as meek as a new-born lamb,
I'm now Sir Murgatroyd—ha! ha!
With greater precision,
(Without the elision)
Sir Ruthven Murgatroyd—ha! ha!

ADAM

And I, who was once his *valley-de-sham,*
As steward I'm now employ'd—ha! ha!
The dickens may take him—
I'll never forsake him!
As steward I'm now employ'd—ha! ha!

BOTH

How dreadful when an innocent heart
Becomes, perforce, a bad young Bart.,
And still more hard on old Adam
His former faithful *valley-de-sham,*
His former faithful *valley-de-sham,*

SIR RUTHVEN	**ADAM**
His *valley-de-sham,*	His *valley-de-sham*
	His *valley-de-sham,*
His *valley-de-sham,* de-sham!	His *valley,* his *valley-de-sham!*

SIR RUTHVEN   This is a painful state of things, Old Adam!

ADAM   Painful, indeed! Ah, my poor master, when I swore that, come what would, I would serve you in all things for ever, I little thought to what a pass it would bring me! The confidential adviser to the greatest villain unhung! Now, Sir, to business. What crime do you propose to commit to-day?

SIR RUTHVEN	How should I know? As my confidential adviser, it's your duty to suggest something.
ADAM	Sir, I loathe the life you are leading, but a good old man's oath is paramount, and I obey. Richard Dauntless is here with pretty Rose Maybud, to ask your consent to their marriage. Poison their beer.
SIR RUTHVEN	No—not that—I know I'm a bad Bart., but I'm not as bad a Bart. as all that.
ADAM	Well, there you are, you see! It's no use my making suggestions if you don't adopt them.
SIR RUTHVEN	(*melodramatically*) How would it be, do you think, were I to lure him here with cunning wile—bind him with good stout rope to yonder post—and then, by making hideous faces at him, curdle the heart-blood in his arteries, and freeze the very marrow in his bones? How say you, Adam, is not the scheme well planned?
ADAM	It would be simply rude—nothing more. But soft—they come!

ADAM and SIR RUTHVEN retire up as RICHARD and ROSE enter, preceded by CHORUS OF BRIDESMAIDS.

Music No. 2.	DUET—(Rose and Richard) and CHORUS OF GIRLS
	"Happily coupled are we"
RICHARD	Happily coupled are we, You see— I am a jolly Jack Tar, My star, And you are the fairest, The richest and rarest Of innocent lasses you are, By far— Of innocent lasses you are! Fanned by a favouring gale, You'll sail Over life's treacherous sea With me, And as for bad weather We'll brave it together, And you shall creep under my lee, My wee! And you shall creep under my lee, My wee! For you are such a smart little craft— Such a neat little, sweet little craft. Such a bright little, tight little, Slight little, light little, Trim little, prim little craft!
CHORUS	For she is such a smart little craft— Such a neat little, sweet little craft.

35

CHORUS (Contd.)	Such a bright little, tight little, Slight little, light little, Trim little, prim little craft!
ROSE	My hopes will be blighted I fear, My dear; In a month you'll be going to sea, Quite free, And all of my wishes You'll throw to the fishes As though they were never to be; Poor me! As though they were never to be. And I shall be left all alone To moan, And weep at your cruel deceit, Complete; While you'll be asserting Your freedom by flirting With every woman you meet, You cheat—Ah, With every woman you meet! Ah Though I am such a smart little craft— Such a neat little, sweet little craft. Such a bright little, tight little, Slight little, light little, Trim little, prim little craft!
CHORUS	Though she is such a smart little craft— Such a neat little, sweet little craft, Such a bright little, tight little, Slight little, light little, Trim little, prim little

ROSE & RICHARD	**CHORUS**
Ah! Ah! - - - - - -	craft! Such a bright little, tight little, Slight little, light little, Trim little, prim little craft!

Enter SIR RUTHVEN

SIR RUTHVEN	Soho! pretty one—in my power at last, eh? Know ye not that I have those within my call who, at my lightest bidding, would immure ye in an uncomfortable dungeon? (*Calling*) What ho! within there!
RICHARD	Hold—we are prepared for this (*producing a Union Jack*) Here is a flag that none dare defy (*all kneel*), and while this glorious rag floats over Rose Maybud's head, the man does not live who would dare to lay unlicensed hand upon her!
SIR RUTHVEN	Foiled—and by a Union Jack! But a time will come and then—
ROSE	(*to* RICHARD). Nay, let me plead with him (*to* SIR RUTH.). Sir Ruthven, have pity. In my book of etiquette the case of a maiden

ROSE (Contd.)	about to be wedded to one who unexpectedly turns out to be a baronet with a curse on him is not considered. Time was when you loved me madly. Prove that this was no selfish love by according your consent to my marriage with one who, if he be not you yourself, is the next best thing—your dearest friend!
Music No. 3.	SONG—(Rose, with Chorus of Girls, Sir Ruthven and Richard)
	"In bygone days"
ROSE	In bygone days I had thy love— Thou hadst my heart. But Fate, all human vows above, Our lives did part! By the old love thou hadst for me By the fond heart that beat for thee— By joys that never now can be, Grant thou my prayer!
ALL	(*kneeling*). Grant thou her prayer!
SIR RUTHVEN	(*recit.*). Take her—I yield.
ALL	Oh rapture!
CHORUS	Away to the parson we go— Say we're solicitous very That he will turn two into one— Singing hey, derry down derry!
RICHARD	For she *is* such a smart little craft—
ROSE	Such a neat little, sweet little craft—
RICHARD	Such a bright little—
ROSE	Tight little—
RICHARD	Slight little—
ROSE	Light little—
BOTH	Trim little, prim little craft!
CHORUS	For she *is* such a smart little craft, Such a neat little, sweet little craft— Such a bright little, tight little, Slight little, light little, Trim little, prim little

ROSE & RICHARD Ah! Ah! - - - - -	**CHORUS** craft! Such a bright little, tight little, Slight little, light little, Trim little, prim little craft!

[Exeunt all but SIR RUTHVEN.

SIR RUTHVEN   For a week I have fulfilled my accursed doom! I have duly committed a crime a day! Not a great crime, I trust, but still in the eyes of one as strictly regulated as I used to be, a crime. But will my ghostly ancestors be satisfied with what I have done, or will they regard it as an unworthy subterfuge? (*Addressing Pictures*) Oh, my forefathers, wallowers in blood, there came at last a day when, sick of crime, you, each and every, vowed to sin no more, and so, in agony, called welcome Death to free you from your cloying guiltiness. Let the sweet psalm of that repentant hour soften your long-dead hearts, and tune your souls to mercy on your poor posterity! (*kneeling*).

(*The stage darkens for a moment. It becomes light again, and the Pictures are seen to have become animated.*)

Music No. 4.   CHORUS OF ANCESTORS, with SOLOS—(Sir Ruthven and Sir Roderic)

"Painted emblems"

CHORUS OF FAMILY PORTRAITS

Painted emblems of a race,
All accurst in days of yore,
Each from his accustomed place
Steps into the world once more.

(*The Pictures step from their frames and march round the stage.*)

Baronet of Ruddigore,
Last of our accursèd line,
Down upon the oaken floor—
Down upon those knees of thine.

Coward, poltroon, shaker, squeamer,
Blockhead, sluggard, dullard, dreamer,
Shirker, shuffler, crawler, creeper,
Sniffler, snuffler, wailer, weeper,
Earthworm, maggot, tadpole, weevil!
Set upon thy course of evil
Lest the King of Spectre-Land
Set on thee his grisly hand!

(*The Spectre of* SIR RODERIC *descends from his frame.*)

SIR RODERIC   Beware! beware! beware!

SIR RUTHVEN   Gaunt vision, who art thou
That thus, with icy glare
And stern relentless brow,
Appearest, who knows how?

38

SIR RODERIC	I am the spectre of the late Sir Roderic Murgatroyd. Who comes to warn thee that thy fate Thou canst not now avoid.
SIR RUTHVEN	Alas, poor ghost!
SIR RODERIC	The pity you Express, for nothing goes: We spectres are a jollier crew Than you, perhaps, suppose!
CHORUS	We spectres are a jollier crew Than you, perhaps, suppose!
Music No. 5.	SONG—(Sir Roderic) and CHORUS "When the night wind howls"
SIR RODERIC	When the night wind howls in the chimney cowls, and the bat in the moonlight flies, And inky clouds, like funeral shrouds, sail over the midnight skies— When the footpads quail at the night-bird's wail, and black dogs bay at the moon, Then is the spectre's holiday— then is the ghost's high noon!

SIR RODERIC	**CHORUS** Ha! Ha!
For then is the ghost's high noon,	 Ha! Ha!
high noon, then is the ghost's high noon!	high noon, then is the ghost's high noon!

SIR RODERIC	As the sob of the breeze sweeps over the trees and the mists lie low on the fen, From grey tomb-stones are gathered the bones that once were women and men, And away they go, with a mop and a mow, to the revel that ends too soon, For cock crow limits our holiday— the dead of the night's high noon!

SIR RODERIC	**CHORUS** Ha! Ha!
The dead of the night's high noon,	 Ha! Ha!
high noon, the dead of the night's high noon!	high noon, the dead of the night's high noon!

SIR RODERIC	And then each ghost with his ladye-toast to their church-yard beds take flight, With a kiss, perhaps, on her lantern chaps,

SIR RODERIC (Contd.)	and a grisly grim "good night!" Till the welcome knell of the midnight bell rings forth its jolliest tune, And ushers in our next high holiday— the dead of the night's high noon!

SIR RODERIC	CHORUS
	Ha! Ha!
The dead of the night's high noon,	
	Ha! Ha!
high noon,	high noon,
the dead of the night's high noon!	the dead of the night's high noon! Ha! ha! ha! ha!

SIR RUTHVEN	I recognize you now—you are the Picture that hangs at the end of the gallery.
SIR RODERIC	In a bad light. I am.
SIR RUTHVEN	Are you considered a good likeness?
SIR RODERIC	Pretty well. Flattering.
SIR RUTHVEN	Because as a work of art you are poor.
SIR RODERIC	I am crude in colour, but I have only been painted ten years. In a couple of centuries I shall be an Old Master, and then you will be sorry you spoke lightly of me.
SIR RUTHVEN	And may I ask why you have left your frames?
SIR RODERIC	It is our duty to see that our successors commit their daily crimes in a conscientious and workmanlike fashion. It is our duty to remind you that you are evading the conditions under which you are permitted to exist.
SIR RUTHVEN	Really, I don't know what you'd have. I've only been a bad baronet a week, and I've committed a crime punctually every day.
SIR RODERIC	Let us enquire into this. Monday?
SIR RUTHVEN	Monday was a Bank Holiday.
SIR RODERIC	True. Tuesday?
SIR RUTHVEN	On Tuesday I made a false income-tax return.
ALL	Ha! ha!
1st GHOST	That's nothing.
2nd. GHOST	Nothing at all.
3rd. GHOST	Everybody does that.
4th. GHOST	It's expected of you.

SIR RODERIC	Wednesday?
SIR RUTHVEN	(*melodramatically*). On Wednesday, I forged a will.
SIR RODERIC	Whose will?
SIR RUTHVEN	My own.
SIR RODERIC	My good sir, you can't forge your own will!
SIR RUTHVEN	Can't I though! I like that! I *did!* Besides, if a man can't forge his own will, whose will can he forge?
1st. GHOST	There's something in that.
2nd. GHOST	Yes, it seems reasonable.
3rd. GHOST	At first sight it does.
4th. GHOST	Fallacy somewhere, I fancy!
SIR RUTHVEN	A man can do what he likes with his own?
SIR RODERIC	I suppose he can.
SIR RUTHVEN	Well then, he can forge his own will, stoopid! On Thursday I shot a fox.
1st. GHOST	Hear, hear!
SIR RODERIC	That's better (*addressing Ghosts*). Pass the fox, I think? (*They assent.*) Yes, pass the fox. Friday?
SIR RUTHVEN	On Friday I forged a cheque.
SIR RODERIC	Whose cheque?
SIR RUTHVEN	Old Adam's.
SIR RODERIC	But Old Adam hasn't a banker.
SIR RUTHVEN	I didn't say I forged his banker—I said I forged his cheque. On Saturday I disinherited my only son.
SIR RODERIC	But you haven't got a son.
SIR RUTHVEN	No—not yet. I disinherited him in advance, to save time. You see—by this arrangement—he'll be born ready disinherited.
SIR RODERIC	I see. But I don't think you can do that.
SIR RUTHVEN	My good sir, if I can't disinherit my own unborn son, whose unborn son can I disinherit?

41

SIR RODERIC	Humph! These arguments sound very well, but I can't help thinking that, if they were reduced to syllogistic form, they wouldn't hold water. Now quite understand us. We are foggy, but we don't permit our fogginess to be presumed upon. Unless you undertake to—well, suppose we say, carry off a lady? (*addressing Ghosts.*) Those who are in favour of his carrying off a lady—(*all hold up their hands except a Bishop*). Those of the contrary opinion? (*Bishop holds up his hands.*) Oh, you're never satisfied! Yes, unless you undertake to carry off a lady at once—I don't care what lady—any lady—choose your lady— you perish in inconceivable agonies.
SIR RUTHVEN	Carry off a lady? Certainly not, on any account. I've the greatest respect for ladies, and I wouldn't do anything of the kind for worlds! No, no. I'm not that kind of baronet, I assure you! If that's all you've got to say, you'd better go back to your frames.
SIR RODERIC	Very good—then let the agonies commence.
	GHOSTS make passes. SIR RUTHVEN begins to writhe in agony.
SIR RUTHVEN	Oh! Oh! Don't do that! I can't stand it!
SIR RODERIC	Painful, isn't it? It gets worse by degrees.
SIR RUTHVEN	Oh—oh! Stop a bit! Stop it, will you? I want to speak.
	SIR RODERIC makes signs to GHOSTS, who resume their attitudes.
SIR RODERIC	Better?
SIR RUTHVEN	Yes—better now! Whew!
SIR RODERIC	Well, do you consent?
SIR RUTHVEN	But it's such an ungentlemanly thing to do!
SIR RODERIC	As you please. (*To Ghosts*) Carry on!
SIR RUTHVEN	Stop—I can't stand it! I agree! I promise! It shall be done.
SIR RODERIC	To-day?
SIR RUTHVEN	To-day!
SIR RODERIC	At once?
SIR RUTHVEN	At once! I retract! I apologize! I had no idea it was anything like that!

Music No. 6.   CHORUS

"He yields"

TENORS
He yields! He yields!
He answers to our call!
We do not ask for more.

A sturdy fellow, after all,
This latest Ruddigore!
All perish in unheard of woe
Who dare our wills defy:
We want your pardon, ere we go,

For having agonized you so—
So pardon us—

So pardon us—
Or die!
So pardon us—

So pardon us—
Or die!

BASSES
He yields! He yields!
He answers to our call!
We do not ask for more.
A sturdy fellow, after all,
This latest Ruddigore!

All perish in unheard of woe
Who dare our wills defy:

We want your pardon, ere we go,
For having agonized you so—

So pardon us—

Or die!

So pardon us—
So pardon us—
Or die!

SIR RUTHVEN   I pardon you!
                    I pardon you!

TENORS & BASSES He pardons us,
                     He pardons us,
                     He pardons us—
                     Hurrah!

(The Ghosts return to their frames)

TENORS & BASSES Painted emblems of a race
                     All accurst in days of yore,
                     Each to his accustomed place
                     Steps unwillingly, once more!

By this time the GHOSTS have changed to pictures again.
SIR RUTHVEN is overcome by emotion.

Enter ADAM.

ADAM   My poor master, you are not well—

SIR RUTHVEN Adam, it won't do—I've seen 'em—all my ancestors—they're just
gone. They say that I must do something desperate at once, or perish
in horrible agonies. Go—go to yonder village—carry off a maiden—
bring her here at once—any one—I don't care which—

43

ADAM	But—
SIR RUTHVEN	Not a word, but obey! Fly!
	Exeunt SIR RUTHVEN *and* ADAM.
	Enter DESPARD *and* MARGARET. *They are both dressed in sober black of formal cut, and present a strong contrast to their appearance in Act I.*
Music No. 7.	DUET—(Margaret and Despard)
	"I once was a very"
DESPARD	I once was a very abandoned person—
MARGARET	Making the most of evil chances.
DESPARD	Nobody could conceive a worse 'un—
MARGARET	Even in all the old romances.
DESPARD	I blush for my wild extravagances, But be so kind To bear in mind,
MARGARET	We were the victims of circumstances! (*Dance.*) That is one of our blameless dances.
MARGARET	I was once an exceedingly odd young lady—
DESPARD	Suffering much from spleen and vapours.
MARGARET	Clergymen thought my conduct shady—
DESPARD	She didn't spend much upon linen-drapers.
MARGARET	It certainly entertain'd the gapers My ways were strange Beyond all range—
DESPARD	Paragraphs got into all the papers. (*Dance*) We only cut respectable capers.
DESPARD	I've given up all my wild proceedings.
MARGARET	My taste for a wand'ring life is waning
DESPARD	Now I'm a dab at penny readings.
MARGARET	They are not remarkably entertaining.

44

DESPARD	A moderate livelihood we're gaining.
MARGARET	In fact we rule A National School.
DESPARD	The duties are dull, but I'm not complaining. (*Dance*) This sort of thing takes a deal of training!
DESPARD	We have been married a week.
MARGARET	One happy, happy week!
DESPARD	Our new life—
MARGARET	Is delightful indeed!
DESPARD	So calm!
MARGARET	So unimpassioned! (*wildly*) Master, all this I owe to you! See, I am no longer wild and untidy. My hair is combed. My face is washed. My boots fit!
DESPARD	Margaret, don't. Pray restrain yourself. Remember, you are now a district visitor.
MARGARET	A gentle district visitor.
DESPARD	You are orderly, methodical, neat; you have your emotions well under control.
MARGARET	I have! (*wildly*.) Master, when I think of all you have done for me, I fall at your feet. I embrace your ankles. I hug your knees! (*Doing so.*)
DESPARD	Hush. This is not well. This is calculated to provoke remark. Be composed, I beg!
MARGARET	Ah! you are angry with poor little Mad Margaret!
DESPARD	No, not angry; but a district visitor should learn to eschew melodrama. Visit the poor, by all means, and give them tea and barley-water, but don't do it as if you were administering a bowl of deadly nightshade. It upsets them. Then when you nurse sick people, and find them not as well as could be expected, why go into hysterics?
MARGARET	Why not?
DESPARD	Because it's too jumpy for a sick-room.
MARGARET	How strange! Oh, Master! Master!—how shall I express the all-absorbing gratitude that—(*about to throw herself at his feet*).
DESPARD	Now! (*warmingly*).

45

MARGARET	Yes, I know, dear—it sha'n't occur again. (*He is seated—she sits on the ground by him*). Shall I tell you one of poor Mad Margaret's odd thoughts? Well, then, when I am lying awake at night, and the pale moonlight streams through the latticed casement, strange fancies crowd upon my poor mad brain, and I sometimes think that if we could hit upon some word for you to use whenever I am about to relapse—some word that teems with hidden meaning—like "Basingstoke"—it might recall me to my saner self. For, after all, I am only Mad Margaret! Daft Meg! Poor Peg! He! he! he!
DESPARD	Poor child, she wanders! But soft—someone comes—Margaret—pray recollect yourself—Basingstoke, I beg! Margaret, if you don't Basingstoke at once, I shall be seriously angry.
MARGARET	(*recovering herself*). Basingstoke it is!
DESPARD	Then make it so.

Enter SIR RUTHVEN. He starts on seeing them.

SIR RUTHVEN	(*aside*). Despard! And his young wife! (*Aloud.*) This visit is unexpected.
MARGARET	Shall I fly at him? Shall I tear him limb from limb? Shall I rend him asunder? Say but the word and—
DESPARD	Basingstoke!
MARGARET	(*suddenly demure*). Basingstoke it is!
DESPARD	(*aside*). Then make it so. (*Aloud*). My brother—I call you brother still, despite your horrible profligacy—we have come to urge you to abandon the evil courses to which you have committed yourself, and at any cost to become a pure and blameless ratepayer.
SIR RUTHVEN	But I've done no wrong yet.
MARGARET	(*wildly*). No wrong! He has done no wrong! Did you hear that!
DESPARD	Basingstoke.
MARGARET	(*recovering herself*). Basingstoke it is.
DESPARD	My brother—I still call you brother, you observe—you forget that you have been, in the eye of the law, a Bad Baronet of Ruddigore for ten years—and you are therefore responsible—in the eye of the law—for all the misdeeds committed by the unhappy gentleman who occupied your place.
SIR RUTHVEN	I see! Bless my heart, I never thought of that! Was I very bad?
DESPARD	Awful. Wasn't he? (*to MARGARET*).

SIR RUTHVEN	And I've been going on like this for how long?
DESPARD	Ten years! Think of all the atrocities you have committed—by attorney as it were—during that period. Remember how you trifled with this poor child's affections—how you raised her hopes on high (don't cry, my love—Basingstoke, you know), only to trample them in the dust when they were at the very zenith of their fulness. Oh fie, sir, fie—she trusted you!
SIR RUTHVEN	Did she? What a scoundrel I must have been! There, there—don't cry, my dear (*to* MARGARET, *who is sobbing on* SIR RUTHVEN'S *breast*), it's all right now. Birmingham, you know—Birmingham—
MARGARET	(*sobbing*). It's Ba—Ba—Basingstoke!
SIR RUTHVEN	Basingstoke! of course it is—Basingstoke.
MARGARET	Then make it so!
SIR RUTHVEN	There, there—it's all right—he's married you now—that is, *I've* married you (*turning to* DESPARD)—I say, which of us has married her?
DESPARD	Oh, *I've* married her.
SIR RUTHVEN	(*aside*). Oh, I'm glad of that (*to* MARGARET). Yes *he's* married you now (*passing her over to* DESPARD), and anything more disreputable than my conduct seems to have been I've never even heard of. But my mind is made up—I *will* defy my ancestors. I *will* refuse to obey their behests, thus, by courting death, atone in some degree for the infamy of my career!
MARGARET	I knew it—I knew it—God bless you—(*hysterically*).
DESPARD	Basingstoke!
MARGARET	Basingstoke it is! (*Recovers herself.*)
Music No. 8.	TRIO—(Margaret, Sir Ruthven, and Despard) "My eyes are fully open"
SIR RUTHVEN	My eyes are fully open to my awful situation— I shall go at once to Roderic and make him an oration. I shall tell him I've recovered my forgotten moral senses, And I don't care two-pence halfpenny for any consequences. Now I do not want to perish by the sword or by the dagger, But a martyr may indulge a little pardonable swagger, And a word or two of compliment my vanity would flatter, But I've got to die to-morrow, so it really doesn't matter!

47

MARGARET

So it really doesn't matter,
matter, matter, matter, matter—
So it really doesn't matter—

DESPARD
So it really doesn't matter,
matter, matter, matter, matter—
So it really doesn't matter,
matter, matter, matter, matter—

SIR RUTHVEN   So it really doesn't matter!

DESPARD   So it really doesn't matter!

MARGARET
So it really doesn't matter,
matter, matter, matter, matter!

SIR RUTHVEN & DESPARD
So it really doesn't matter,
matter, matter, matter, matter,
matter, matter, matter, matter, matter
matter, matter, matter, mat-
ter, matter, matter, matter, matter,
matter!

If I were not a little mad and
generally silly

MARGARET   I should give you my advice upon the subject, willy
nilly;
I should show you in a moment how to grapple with the
question,
And you'd really be astonished at the force of my
suggestion.
On the subject I shall write you a most valuable letter,
Full of excellent suggestions when I feel a little better,
But at present I'm afraid I am as mad as any hatter,
So I'll keep 'em to myself, for my opinion doesn't
matter!

SIR RUTHVEN

Her opinion doesn't matter,
matter, matter, matter, matter,
Her opinion doesn't matter!

DESPARD
Her opinion doesn't matter,
matter, matter, matter, matter,
Her opinion doesn't matter,
matter, matter, matter, matter!

MARGARET   My opinion doesn't matter,

DESPARD   Her opinion doesn't matter,

MARGARET & SIR RUTH

My ⎫
Her ⎭ opinion doesn't matter,

matter, matter, matter, matter,
matter, matter, matter, matter, matter,
matter, matter, matter, mat-
ter, matter, matter, matter, matter,
matter!

DESPARD

Her opinion doesn't matter,

matter, matter, matter, matter!

If I had been so lucky as to
have a steady brother

DESPARD   Who could talk to me as we are talking now to one
another—
Who could give me good advice when he discovered I
was erring,
(Which is just the very favour which on you I am
conferring),

DESPARD (Contd.)   My existence would have made a rather interesting idyll,
And I might have lived and died a very decent indiwiddle.
This particularly rapid, unintelligible patter
Isn't generally heard, and if it is it doesn't matter!

SIR RUTHVEN   If it is it doesn't matter,

MARGARET	**SIR RUTHVEN**
If it is it doesn't matter,	matter, matter, matter, matter,
matter, matter, matter, matter,	If it is it doesn't matter,
If it is it doesn't matter!	matter, matter, matter, matter!

ALL THREE   This particularly rapid, unintelligible patter
Isn't generally heard, and if it is it doesn't matter,
This particularly rapid, unintelligible patter
Isn't generally heard, and if it is it doesn't matter,
matter, matter, matter, matter, matter,
matter, matter, matter, matter, matter!

(Exeunt DESPARD and MARGARET)

Enter ADAM

ADAM   (*guiltily*). Master—the deed is done!

SIR RUTHVEN   What deed?

ADAM   She is here—alone, unprotected—

SIR RUTHVEN   Who?

ADAM   The maiden. I've carried her off—I had a hard task, for she fought like a tiger-cat!

SIR RUTHVEN   Great heaven, I had forgotten her! I had hoped to have died unspotted by crime, but I am foiled again—and by a tiger-cat! Produce her—and leave us!

(ADAM introduces OLD HANNAH, very much excited, and exit.)

Music No. 9.   MELODRAME

SIR RUTHVEN   Dame Hannah! This is—this is not what I expected.

HANNAH   Well, sir, and what would you with me? Oh, you have begun bravely— bravely indeed! Unappalled by the calm dignity of blameless womanhood, your minion has torn me from my spotless home, and dragged me, blindfold and shrieking, through hedges, over stiles, and across a very difficult country, and left me, helpless, and trembling, at your mercy! Yet not helpless, coward sir, for approach one step—nay, but the twentieth part of one poor inch—and this poniard (*produces a very small dagger*) shall teach ye what it is to lay unholy hands on old Stephen Trusty's daughter!

SIR RUTHVEN	Madam, I am extremely sorry for this. It is not at all what I intended—anything more correct—more deeply respectful than my intentions towards you, it would be impossible for anyone—however particular—to desire.
HANNAH	Bah, I am not to be tricked by smooth words, hypocrite! But be warned in time, for there are, without, a hundred gallant hearts whose trusty blades would hack him limb from limb who dared to lay unholy hands on old Stephen Trusty's daughter!
SIR RUTHVEN	And this is what it is to embark upon a career of unlicensed pleasure!
	(HANNAH, who has taken a formidable dagger from one of the armed figures, throws her small dagger to SIR RUTHVEN).
HANNAH	Harkye, miscreant, you have secured me, and I am your poor prisoner; but if you think I cannot take care of myself you are very much mistaken. Now then, it's one to one, and let the best man win!
	(Making for him.)
SIR RUTHVEN	(*in an agony of terror*) Don't! don't look at me like that! I can't bear it! Roderic! Uncle! Save me!
	SIR RODERIC enters, from his picture. He comes down the stage.
SIR RODERIC	What is the matter? Have you carried her off?
SIR RUTHVEN	I have—she is there—look at her—she terrifies me!
SIR RODERIC	(*Looking at* HANNAH). Little Nannikin!
HANNAH	(*amazed*). Roddy-doddy!
SIR RODERIC	My own old love! Why, how came *you* here?
HANNAH	This brute—he carried me off! Bodily! But I'll show him! (*about to rush at* SIR RUTHVEN).
SIR RODERIC	Stop! (*to* SIR RUTHVEN). What do you mean by carrying off this lady? Are you aware that, once upon a time, she was engaged to be married to me? I'm very angry—very angry indeed.
SIR RUTHVEN	Now I hope this will be a lesson to you in future, not to—
SIR RODERIC	Hold your tongue, sir.
SIR RUTHVEN	Yes, uncle.
SIR RODERIC	Have you given him any encouragement?

HANNAH	(*to* SIR RUTHVEN). Have I given you any encouragement? Frankly now, have I?
SIR RUTHVEN	No. Frankly, you have not. Anything more scrupulously correct than your conduct, it would be impossible to desire.
SIR RODERIC	You go away.
SIR RUTHVEN	Yes, uncle. [*Exit* SIR RUTHVEN.
SIR RODERIC	This is a strange meeting after so many years!
HANNAH	Very. I thought you were dead.
SIR RODERIC	I am. I died ten years ago.
HANNAH	And are you pretty comfortable?
SIR RODERIC	Pretty well—that is—yes, pretty well.
HANNAH	You don't deserve to be, for I loved you all the while, dear; and it made me dreadfully unhappy to hear of all your goings on, you bad, bad boy!
Music No. 10.	SONG—HANNAH (with Sir Roderic) "There grew a little flower"
HANNAH	There grew a little flower 'Neath a great oak tree: When the tempest 'gan to lower Little heeded she: No need had she to cower, For she dreaded not its power— She was happy in the bower Of her great oak tree! Sing hey, Lack-a-day! Sing hey, Lack-a-day Let the tears fall free For the pretty little flower and the great oak tree!

HANNAH	**SIR RODERIC**
Sing hey,	
Lack-a-day!	Sing hey,
Sing hey,	Lack-a-day!
Lack-a-day!	Sing hey,
Sing	Lack-a-day!
hey lack-a-day!	Hey, lack-a-day!

51

BOTH	Let the tears fall free For the pretty little flower and the great oak tree!
HANNAH	When she found that he was fickle, Was that great oak tree, She was in a pretty pickle, As she well might be— But his gallantries were mickle, For Death followed with his sickle, And her tears began to trickle For her great oak tree! Sing hey, Lack-a-day! Sing hey, Lack-a-day Let the tears fall free For the pretty little flower and the great oak tree!

HANNAH	**SIR RODERIC**
Sing hey,	
	Sing hey,
Lack-a-day!	
	Lack-a-day!
Sing hey,	
	Sing hey,
Lack-a-day!	
	Lack-a-day!
Sing hey, lack-a-day!	
	Hey, lack-a-day!

BOTH	Let the tears fall free For the pretty little flower and the great oak tree!
HANNAH	Said she, "He loved me never, Did that great oak tree, But I'm neither rich nor clever, And so why should he? But though fate our fortunes sever, To be constant I'll endeavour, Aye, for ever and for ever, To my great oak tree!" Sing hey, Lack-a-day! Sing hey, Lack-a-day Let the tears fall free For the pretty little flower and the great oak tree!

HANNAH	**SIR RODERIC**
Sing hey,	
	Sing hey,
Lack-a-day!	
	Lack-a-day!
Sing hey,	
	Sing hey,

HANNAH (Contd.) Lack-a-day! Sing hey, lack-a-day!	**SIR RODERIC** (Contd.) Lack-a-day! Hey, lack-a-day!

BOTH Let the tears fall free
For the pretty little flower and the great oak tree!

(HANNAH falls weeping on SIR RODERIC's bosom.)

HANNAH Sing hey, Lack-a-day! Hey, lack-a-day, lack-a-day, lack-a-day!	**SIR RODERIC** Sing hey, Lack-a-day! Hey, lack-a-day, lack-a-day! lack-a-day!

Enter SIR RUTHVEN, excitedly, followed by all the characters and CHORUS OF BRIDESMAIDS and BUCKS and BLADES.

SIR RUTHVEN Stop a bit—both of you.

SIR RODERIC This intrusion is unmannerly.

HANNAH I'm surprised at you.

SIR RUTHVEN I can't stop to apologize—an idea has just occurred to me. A Baronet of Ruddigore can only die through refusing to commit his daily crime.

SIR RODERIC No doubt.

SIR RUTHVEN Therefore, to refuse to commit a daily crime is tantamount to suicide!

SIR RODERIC It would seem so.

SIR RUTHVEN But suicide is, itself, a crime—and so, by your own showing, you ought never to have died at all!

SIR RODERIC I see—I understand! Then I'm practically alive!

SIR RUTHVEN Undoubtedly! (SIR RODERIC *embraces* HANNAH.) Rose, when you believed that I was a simple farmer, I believe you loved me?

ROSE Madly, passionately!

SIR RUTHVEN But when I became a bad baronet, you very properly loved Richard instead?

ROSE	Passionately, madly!
SIR RUTHVEN	But if I should turn out *not* to be a bad baronet after all, how would you love me then?
ROSE	Madly, passionately!
SIR RUTHVEN	As before?
ROSE	Why, of course!
SIR RUTHVEN	My darling!
	[They embrace.
RICHARD	Here, I say, belay!
ROSE	Oh, sir, belay, if it's absolutely necessary.
SIR RUTHVEN	Belay? Certainly not!
Music No. 11.	FINALE—ACT II
	"Oh, happy the lily when kissed by the bee"
CHORUS	Oh, happy the lily When kiss'd by the bee; And, sipping tranquilly, Quite happy is he; And happy the filly That neighs in her pride;

SOPRANOS	**ALTOS**	**TENORS**	**BASSES**
		But	
But	But	happier than	But
happier than	happier than	a -	happier than
any	any	ny	any
A	A	A	A
pound	pound	pound to a	pound
to a	to a	pen -	to a
penny,	penny,	ny,	penny,
A	A	A	A
lov -	lov -	lover is	lov -
er is,	er is,	when	er is,
when he	when he	he	when he

ALL   Embraces his bride!
Embraces his bride!
Embraces his bride!

CURTAIN